8/09

TEEN LIFE™

FREQUENTLY ASKED QUESTIONS ABOUT

Exercise Addiction

Edward Willett

ROSEN PUBLISHING®

New York

Published in 2009 by The Rosen Publishing Group, Inc.
29 East 21st Street, New York, NY 10010

Copyright © 2009 by The Rosen Publishing Group, Inc.

First Edition

Library of Congress Cataloging-in-Publication Data

Willett, Edward, 1959–
Frequently asked questions about exercise addiction / Edward Willett.—1st ed.
    p. cm.—(FAQ: teen life)
Includes index.
ISBN-13: 978-1-4042-1806-2 (library binding)
1. Exercise addiction—Juvenile literature. 2. Eating disorders—Juvenile literature. I. Title.
RC569.5.E94W55 2009
362.196'8526—dc22

                                                      2008000358

Manufactured in the United States of America

Contents

WHAT IS AN EATING DISORDER?

People with eating disorders are very concerned with the size and shape of their bodies. They think they are too heavy and need to lose weight, even though they are at or below a healthy weight. Because of this, they eat and exercise in unhealthy ways.

The National Eating Disorders Association estimates that approximately eleven million people in the United States struggle with eating disorders that warrant medical treatment. Ninety to 95 percent are women. For many, the problem begins when they are teenagers.

If it becomes severe, an eating disorder can take over a person's life. Unless that person gets help—and wants help—that person may die. According to Anorexia Nervosa and Related Eating Disorders, Inc. (ANRED), 20 percent of people with a serious eating disorder die if they don't get treatment.

Exercise addiction is categorized by most health experts today as a serious eating disorder–related problem. Exercise addiction is also known as compulsive exercise or exercise bulimia.

An eating disorder is a complicated psychological, emotional, and physical problem. Cultural influences can also contribute to an eating disorder. Women experience a lot of pressure from society to be thin and attractive. Some believe this is the reason more women suffer from eating disorders than men. Still, the number of males with eating disorders is increasing.

The two main eating disorders are anorexia nervosa and bulimia nervosa. Compulsive eating (also referred to as binge eating disorder) is also a serious problem. Compulsive exercise is currently classified as a serious eating disorder–related problem, and many experts believe the number of people suffering from it is growing. Compulsive exercise is also called exercise bulimia or exercise addiction.

Each of these disorders is a different type of behavior, but most people with eating disorders suffer from symptoms that fall into more than one category. In other words, many people have symptoms of anorexia and bulimia, or bulimia and exercise addiction, or any combination of the four disorders.

Anorexia Nervosa

The best-known eating disorder is probably anorexia nervosa (usually called anorexia). Although the word "anorexia" means "loss of appetite," the opposite is true. Those with anorexia are hungry all the time. People suffering from anorexia starve themselves in order to lose weight. Those with anorexia fear putting on weight and often see themselves as heavier than they really are. The condition usually begins gradually. They will make certain foods off limits and will eat only specific amounts of food. As time goes on, the list of foods they permit themselves to eat grows shorter. This behavior is called restricted eating. People with anorexia will also fast, which means they will go for long periods of time without eating. Eventually, they lose dangerous, unhealthy amounts of weight. One of the factors used by many doctors to diagnose someone as having anorexia is if that person weighs 15 percent less than the normal body weight for his or her height and age.

Anorexia causes many physical problems. Because the body has so little fat, it can't maintain a normal body temperature.

People with anorexia are frequently cold, even in summer. Young women with anorexia suffer from amenorrhea, which means that menstrual periods stop. Near-starvation and the resulting lack of calcium may cause osteoporosis later in life. Starvation also weakens the heart, which can develop a slow or irregular beat. Loss of fluids can cause dehydration. Dehydration can lead to an electrolyte imbalance in the body, causing death.

Anorexia also causes emotional problems. Because people who have anorexia tend to isolate themselves from family and friends, they may suffer from depression. Lack of food can harm the person's ability to think straight and concentrate. It can also cause a person to feel irritable, unhappy, and pessimistic most of the time.

Bulimia Nervosa

People suffering from bulimia nervosa (commonly called bulimia) make themselves vomit in order to get rid of what they have eaten. They may also use (and abuse) laxatives, drugs, or diuretics (pills that increase urination) that cause vomiting or diarrhea—anything to get the food out of their bodies. This behavior is called purging. Some people with bulimia starve themselves and then throw up what little they do eat. Others eat huge amounts of food in a short period of time—called bingeing—then make themselves vomit. This cycle is often called binge and purge. Some people with bulimia also use excessive exercise or fasting to lose weight.

Bulimia causes many health problems as well. These include dry skin and hair, brittle nails, or bleeding gums. The teeth develop cavities or ragged edges from stomach acids brought

Many teens who have bulimia develop a binge and purge eating cycle. They eat large amounts of food in a short time and then cause themselves to vomit before their bodies have been able to absorb the food's nutrients.

up by frequent vomiting. Vomiting also puts tremendous strain on the stomach and esophagus. When the lining of the esophagus breaks down, an ulcer develops. Purging gets rid of food before nutrients are absorbed. Without these nutrients, the body can suffer from malnutrition.

In addition, repeated use of laxatives can cause painful constipation (an inability to have bowel movements). Abusing diuretics can cause dehydration. Using ipecac syrup to induce vomiting is extremely dangerous and can cause congestive heart failure and death.

Bulimia can cause the same emotional problems that people with anorexia develop. Because people who suffer from bulimia keep their binge/purge cycles a secret, they can feel isolated and alone and suffer from depression. Anorexia Nervosa and Related Eating Disorders, Inc. (ANRED), reported that 50 percent of those who suffer from anorexia develop bulimia. About one million of the eleven million people who suffer from anorexia and bulimia are male.

Compulsive Eating

People with compulsive eating disorder (also called binge eating disorder) eat large amounts of food but don't purge it from their bodies like those who have bulimia. Everyone overeats occasionally, but people with compulsive eating disorder do it frequently. They eat huge amounts of food very quickly whether or not they feel hungry. Some compulsive eaters graze, eating many times during the day or night. Compulsive overeaters usually have their binges in private. They feel unable to control what or how much they eat. Afterward, they feel depressed, guilty, and disgusted with themselves. Compulsive eating is different from the other eating disorders because the person is not trying to lose weight.

Compulsive eating is psychologically damaging because people use food as a way to deal with uncomfortable feelings. Because they may not feel safe expressing sadness, anger, or other emotions, they eat as a way to find comfort. Also, most people with this disorder are overweight and may be at risk for other health problems, such as heart disease and diabetes. Being overweight alone does not always cause health problems, but it can be a problem when combined with an inactive lifestyle. According to the National Institutes of Health, more than four million people have binge eating disorder; almost 40 percent of these individuals are male.

Compulsive Exercise

Compulsive exercise is characterized by using exercise to get rid of calories. This behavior is also known as exercise bulimia because the person is using exercise to purge calories from his or her system. The compulsive exerciser might also eat compulsively, restrict food, throw up, and/or take laxatives, diet pills, or other drugs, or any combination of these.

Compulsive exercise is also a bit different from other eating disorders: it can be a lot easier to hide. If a person stops eating, his or her parents and friends will probably become worried. But because exercise is usually a positive, worthwhile activity, people who stick to an exercise routine are often praised for their discipline. The behavior that wins compliments may actually be harmful. When exercise takes over your life, when it isolates you, when it becomes the sole focus of your thoughts, then it has become unhealthy.

What Is a Negative Body Image?

What do you see when you look in the mirror? The reflection of a happy, healthy young person? Or someone you automatically cut down as too fat, too short, or too ugly? Have you ever thought your whole life would be better if you were thinner and more attractive? These feelings are examples of negative body image.

In today's society, body image is more than just the mental picture you have of what your body looks like. For many, body image is also a reflection of how they feel about themselves and their lives. People with a negative body image believe that if

Many people who are addicted to exercise also restrict the food that they eat. They may take laxatives, diet pills, or other drugs to help them purge calories from their bodies because their fear of gaining weight takes over their lives.

they don't look right, other things, such as their personality, intelligence, social skills, or capabilities, also aren't right. They think that if they fix their bodies, all their other problems will disappear. This can result in unhealthy weight management practices and an unhealthy relationship with food. People excessively diet and exercise out of fear of gaining weight.

Your body image is influenced by many different things. It is influenced by family, friends, and a culture that is obsessed with weight, body shape, dieting, and food. All people have negative thoughts and feelings about their body at some point in their life.

But when it becomes more than a passing concern, when people base their happiness and self-worth on what they eat, how often they exercise, and how much they weigh, they are suffering from a negative body image. This outlook causes people to believe that all their experiences in life are affected by their appearance and body weight.

The problems surrounding body image can be especially difficult for teens. Adolescence is a time when you may feel confused about the changes happening to your body. These changes are a natural part of growing up, but they can make you feel out of control and unhappy with your appearance. As a result, you may turn to unhealthy eating habits, which can lead to a serious eating disorder. This can seriously damage your physical and emotional health.

Nobody is born with a negative body image. It is something that you learn and that develops over time. As you grow older, your experiences are shaped by the different messages you get from society. Those messages often connect personal success and happiness with being thin and beautiful. If people feel they don't measure up to those ideals of success, then they may disregard any real accomplishments. Having a negative body image can seriously distort the way you look at yourself and your life.

Having a negative body image can be very dangerous if it's not addressed. The good news is, because a negative body image is something you learn, it can also be unlearned.

Do you know how to recognize a negative body image, what the causes and consequences are, and how to overcome a negative body image? If you work on learning to love and respect your body right now, you'll have the time, energy, and willpower to focus on the most important part of your being—who you are inside.

Families and Food

As with many other important issues you encounter, your family has a lot of influence on how you feel about food and your body. As you grow older, food takes on different meanings. Parents tell you what is good to eat and when and how much you should eat. Even though you learn that candy and sweets are bad for you, you receive such foods as rewards for good behavior. These mixed messages about food can create some complex eating problems.

Family behaviors around eating habits can have an impact on body image, especially for females. If you see your mother always worrying about her weight, going on and off diets, it sends a powerful message and may make everybody in the family believe that worrying about weight is normal and expected.

Families can also cause negative body image if parents have unreasonably high expectations for their children. These expectations can make you feel inadequate, depressed, or guilty when they don't match your interests. You may take your frustrations out on your body through dieting or excessive exercise as a way to assert control over your life.

The Ideal

If you are struggling with compulsive exercise or any other eating disorder, remember that you are not alone. Millions of

Teens who have a negative body image frequently have family members who add to their feelings of inadequacy. Their family members may have high expectations for them and the teens may feel guilty or depressed when they can't live up to those high expectations.

Americans suffer from eating disorders. Many others deal with eating and exercise problems that may not be severe enough to be called eating disorders but still put them at risk.

One reason for these behaviors is the American culture's emphasis on physical appearance. Too often, people are judged by how they look, rather than who they are. In movies, in magazines, and on television, happy, successful, beautiful people are young and thin, while overweight people are often portrayed negatively. If you were to believe what you see in the media, you might think everyone in the world was thin. But people come in all shapes and sizes.

Young men and women are bombarded with images of what their bodies are supposed to look like. These images project a body shape that is considered the ideal shape, but it's not a reality. All images in advertisement and print media are actually edited, so people compare themselves not with images of supermodels but with images of bodies that don't exist in reality. Obviously, this sets up an "ideal" that they can never, ever reach. Very few men and women actually look like the ideal, and trying to reach that ideal is dangerous and unhealthy for most people. When people measure themselves against these images, they can feel inadequate, no matter what they look like. Advertising relies on and targets this feeling of inadequacy to sell people products that supposedly improve their appearance.

What is considered the ideal body shape varies from culture to culture and is different at different times. One hundred years ago, a pale and round appearance was considered healthy and attractive because it meant that a person lived well and did not have to work outdoors. Being thin and tan was considered unattractive because this meant a person had limited resources.

Everyone has his or her own natural body type. Just as people differ in height and hair color, they differ in body shape and size. But because everywhere they look they see an ideal for women that is very thin and an ideal for men that is slim and muscular, many men and women think they need to drastically change their bodies.

Puberty is the time when girls become women and boys become men. During puberty, it is normal for females to gain weight. This is part of the natural process of becoming a healthy, adult woman. Unfortunately, many girls are unprepared for these physical changes. All around them are images of very thin women, advertisements for exercise equipment and diet shakes, and magazine articles about how to lose weight. They believe this natural, healthy weight gain is bad, and they begin to diet.

Exercise Enters the Picture

Since the 1980s, Americans have become more aware of the connection between exercise and good health. At the same time, there has also been more of an emphasis on using exercise to change and improve their appearance. Take a look in your favorite magazine. Is there an article about exercise? What does it say? Does it emphasize health benefits, like preventing heart disease and strengthening bones? Does it talk about how and why exercise makes you feel good inside? Or is it about how to get a flat stomach and firm thighs, or how to lose weight? Experts believe that the emphasis on exercise as a weight-loss tool is causing a sharp increase in the number of people who exercise compulsively.

Because exercise is considered admirable and healthy, compulsive exercise is easy to hide. If you told your best friend that you threw up after every meal, your friend might be shocked or upset. But if you told your friend you exercised every day, he or she would admire you for your discipline and commitment. You can see how exercise can become an easily hidden addiction.

There's nothing wrong with wanting to look good. But when you feel that being thin is the most important thing in your life, and you believe that gaining weight is the most awful thing that could happen to you, then it is time to reexamine your priorities.

Common Signs of Eating Disorders

Some common signs of eating disorders include the following:

- Constantly thinking about the size and shape of your body
- Constantly thinking about how much you weigh and weighing yourself repeatedly
- Constantly thinking about food, cooking, and eating
- Eating only certain foods in specific and limited amounts
- Keeping a list of what foods are OK to eat
- Wanting to eat alone, feeling uncomfortable eating with other people
- Not feeling good about yourself unless you are thin—but never being satisfied with how thin you are
- Feeling that you should be exercising more—no matter how much you exercise
- Feeling competitive about dieting—wanting to be the thinnest or the smallest
- Taking diet pills or laxatives
- Continuing to diet, even after you are thin

Exercise addiction is sometimes very easy to hide because most people have great admiration for those who put emphasis on exercise and improving their physical appearance. Learn the signs and dangers of compulsive exercise so that you can make healthy decisions or help others overcome their addiction.

- Purposely losing lots of weight very quickly
- Forcing yourself to throw up
- No longer having your period

If anything on this list describes you, you may have an eating disorder. You don't have to have every symptom on the list to have an eating disorder.

Even after you learn about the dangers of having a negative body image or exercise bulimia, it isn't always easy to prevent it or overcome it. It's hard to ignore or even fight against the negative messages you receive every day. But you are not powerless against this problem. There are many ways to stop the habits and behaviors that contribute to a negative body image or exercise addiction and many ways to help you find peace with your body. It may be the hardest thing you ever do, but it's one of the most important things you'll ever do for yourself.

Changing your body image is a process that you will have to work on for many years, if not the rest of your life. The most important thing to remember is that recovery comes through changing your attitude, not your body. Feeling good about yourself is the key to making healthy decisions about how to care for and celebrate your body.

Change can begin by simply educating yourself—reading books and contacting organizations that deal with the dangers of the beauty ideal, negative body image, and eating disorders. But if your problems are more serious, you will need to seek additional help. There are many organizations and people who can help you. If you need more information or help about eating disorders and related behaviors, a good place to start is to contact your doctor, your school nurse, your guidance counselor, your coach, the Alliance for Eating Disorders Awareness, Anorexia Nervosa and Related Eating Disorders, Inc., or the National Eating Disorders Association.

CHAPTER TWO

WHEN DOES EXERCISE BECOME COMPULSIVE EXERCISE?

Exercise is an important part of staying healthy. The Centers for Disease Control and Prevention, a government agency that studies many health issues, including how nutrition and exercise affect people's health, has proven that exercise reduces the risk of high blood pressure and heart disease, which kill thousands of Americans every year. Girls and women who exercise lessen their odds of getting breast cancer and osteoporosis, a disease that causes bones to weaken and break.

A study compiled by the Women's Sports Foundation and updated in 2005 compared girls who engage in sports and girls who don't. The study found that the girls who participated in some form of aerobic exercise—any activity that gets your heart pumping and

There are many physical and psychological benefits of exercise. Nevertheless, you should not think that doing more exercise is even healthier for your body and mind. You can actually injure your muscles, bones, and connective tissue by exercising too much.

your lungs working hard—were happier, did better in school, and had higher self-esteem than the girls who didn't. Other research studies have yielded similar results.

Exercise has a positive effect on happiness and self-esteem for several reasons. When your body is more physically fit, more oxygen gets to your brain and your heart. Your muscles are stronger and firmer. Also, your metabolism is higher, which means that more of the food you eat turns to energy and less turns to fat. Exercise may also strengthen the immune system, the body's defense system against disease and infection. All of these things make you healthier, and being healthier can make you feel more confident. And, as anyone who has ever gone for a run or worked out at a gym when they were upset or angry knows, exercise relieves stress. Exercising causes a surge in your body's production of endorphins, dopamine, and anandamide, the body's own chemicals that we need to feel happy, confident, and relaxed. Your body releases the endorphins, dopamine, and anandamide during and after exercise. Many people find that when they exercise regularly, they sleep better, have more energy, and are less likely to feel depressed.

In addition to the physical benefits of exercise, playing sports, especially team sports, can have psychological benefits. When you play sports, you learn to be more assertive, to compete, and to work as a team. These skills are part of having healthy self-esteem.

But just because exercise is healthy, it doesn't mean that more exercise is even healthier. Experts recommend that people burn between 2,000 and 3,500 calories each week in aerobic exercise—running, jogging, dancing, brisk walking, etc.—to maintain cardiovascular health. You can do thirty-minute exercise sessions six days each week or less strenuous activity an hour every day five days each week. But burning more than 3,500 calories per week results in fewer health benefits and an increased risk of injury.

Similarly, building and maintaining muscle and bone mass requires weight-bearing exercise, but overdoing weight-bearing exercise can tear down muscle tissue and damage bones and joints and connective tissue such as cartilage (the soft tissue in the joints), tendons, and ligaments.

It is possible to exercise too much and for the wrong reasons. Some people become addicted to exercise. This addiction is called compulsive exercise. When people become addicted to exercise, they no longer receive its positive benefits. Instead, their exercise is unhealthy. And, like an addiction to alcohol, cocaine, or any other drug, an addiction to exercise can destroy your life.

People who exercise compulsively feel that they must work out—not because they want to but because they have to. They use exercise as a way to purge calories from their bodies.

People often start exercising because they want to lose weight. Or they may be going through a difficult time in their lives, and exercise helps relieve the tension. But if their self-image gets connected to their ability to exercise, they begin to base their value as human beings on how much they work out.

Discipline or Danger?

Exercise becomes compulsive when people feel worthless and guilty if they don't exercise. To feel good about themselves, they must work out every day. Anyone who exercises regularly has discipline and commitment. But there's a difference between having a commitment to your exercise routine and being excessively rigid about it. Healthy exercisers are committed to exercise, but if they have to skip a few days or weeks or change their routine, they make the adjustment without having a bad day or thinking they're worthless. If compulsive exercisers are forced to change or stop their exercise routine for any reason, they become angry, depressed, or stressed out. That is why they will run even if the weather makes it dangerous to do so. They will take an aerobics class with a torn muscle. If their friends are going to the beach at a time when they usually exercise, compulsive

Addictive exercisers often become angry, stressed out, or depressed if they have to change or halt their exercise regimen. To them, exercise is more important than spending time with their family or friends.

exercisers will make up excuses and go to the gym. To compulsive exercisers, exercise is much more important than a social life.

Compulsive exercisers think that they must exercise every single day to stay the same shape and size. If they are forced to miss one work-out, they imagine that their muscles have become soft or that they've gained weight. They never feel satisfied with how their bodies look.

A Checklist: Is Your Exercise Routine Becoming Compulsive?

This checklist can help you tell if your healthy exercise routine is becoming compulsive. If you check off any of these statements, you're probably exercising for the wrong reasons. If you check off three or more statements, please consider getting help.

➡ I exercise even if I don't feel well or I'm injured. I'll feel better once I get moving.

➡ I become depressed or upset if I miss a workout.

➡ I figure out how much to exercise based on how much I ate. If I eat more, I exercise more.

➡ I lie to my friends and turn down dates or invitations from friends and family rather than change my exercise routine.

➡ I have good days or bad days according to whether or not I've exercised.

➡ I have trouble sitting still because I think I'm not burning calories.

➡ If I don't exercise one day, I think I've gotten bigger or my muscles have gotten soft.

➡ Friends and family complain that I exercise too much.

➡ I've had to drop activities to fit in more exercise.

➡ I sometimes lie about how much or how often I exercise.

➡ I feel content only when I am exercising or within the hour after exercising.

➡ I like exercise better than any other activity—in fact, there's almost nothing I'd rather do.

➡ In addition to my regular schedule, I'll exercise more if I find extra time.

➡ I have a history (or a family history) of anxiety or depression.

It's important to remember that even the most extreme eating disorder usually begins as a mild one. It can be very difficult for someone with an eating disorder to admit—especially to themselves—that they have a problem. If you suspect you have

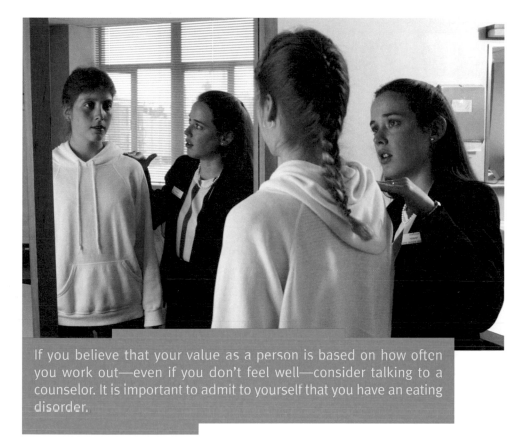

If you believe that your value as a person is based on how often you work out—even if you don't feel well—consider talking to a counselor. It is important to admit to yourself that you have an eating disorder.

an eating disorder, please consider speaking to someone about it. Tell someone you trust—a teacher, a relative, your best friend— that you are concerned. Or go to a counseling center and talk to a counselor. You are not alone, and you can get help.

Myths and Facts

 Myth **Exercise addiction and eating disorders aren't really serious.** Fact ➤ Exercise addiction is an eating disorder–related problem. Eating disorders have the second-highest fatality rate of the psychological disorders.

 Myth **Compulsive exercisers stop exercising when they become ill or injured.** Fact ➤ People who are addicted to exercise will continue to exercise even after they become sick or have a serious injury like a stress fracture.

 Myth **I can fix myself, and stop whenever I want to.** Fact ➤ Eating disorders are very difficult to treat. Treatment typically takes several years to be effective, and in 20 percent of cases, it doesn't work at all.

 **Myth** **I'll be really healthy if I exercise all the time.** Fact ➤ Your body needs time to rebuild itself after exercise. Too much exercise damages

the body instead of strengthening it. Too much exercise in females can lead to amenorrhea (stopping of menstruation) and osteoporosis (causing brittle bones). Some girls who play sports are sometimes at risk for getting female athlete triad, which is a combination of amenorrhea, osteoporosis, and an eating disorder.

Eating disorders are very rare. Fact ➤ It's estimated that in the United States, ten million females and one million males will suffer from an eating disorder at some time in their lives.

Men don't develop eating disorders. Fact ➤ According to Anorexia Nervosa and Related Eating Disorders, Inc. (ANRED), a 2001 report indicated that for every four females who have anorexia, there is one male who has it. For every eight to eleven females with bulimia, one male has that disorder, and binge eating disorder occurs nearly equally among males and females.

WHY DO PEOPLE DEVELOP EATING DISORDERS?

There is no easy answer to why people develop eating disorders. Eating disorders are complex problems. They are caused by a combination of many factors—psychological issues, biological issues, family influences, and messages from society. Also, there is often a "trigger"— a disturbing event in a person's life that he or she responds to with excessive diet and/or exercise. Most eating disorders have several causes, but the person with an eating disorder is not aware of them.

Psychological Factors

A large part of eating disorders is psychological. People who suffer from eating disorders tend to be perfectionists. No matter what they do—get excellent grades, have many talents and abilities, have a full social calendar—they still feel inadequate. Perfection is an unrealistic goal.

Many people who suffer from eating disorder–related problems such as exercise addiction are perfectionists. They feel inadequate or frustrated if other people don't like them, and these feelings can trigger their unhealthy eating or exercise habits.

People with eating disorders may get angry and upset, but they don't feel safe or know how to express their feelings. They are very concerned with pleasing people and being liked. They're afraid that if they show anger, people won't like them.

Family Factors

People with eating disorders tend to have family problems. Their home lives are often unstable or full of disruptions, such as a parent who gets divorced and remarried, or a family that moves from city to city. The eating disorder becomes a way of dealing with stress by giving the person a sense of control over his or her life.

Or a family may be overprotective and the children are not allowed to make their own decisions. Teens may feel their weight is something they can be in charge of. People with eating disorders also may come from families where feelings are not discussed openly, and it is considered wrong to express anger or hurt feelings.

Many people with eating disorders have been physically, emotionally, or sexually abused. In this case, the eating disorder can be a cry for help. It can be a way to bury feelings of shame and guilt and to deal with emotional pain. People who are sexually abused grow up with little or no sense of control over their own bodies and their lives. By rigidly controlling their weight, they may be trying to regain a feeling of control over themselves.

Eating disorders will slow, or even prevent, development into adulthood. A girl with an eating disorder stops getting her period, and her breasts and hips shrink. A boy with an eating disorder will stop producing testosterone. This decreases sexual desire and performance. For a girl or boy who has been sexually abused the developing body may be a reminder of his or her pain and fear. In that case, an eating disorder may express a wish to appear sexually unattractive—to try to stay safe from the abuse and to avoid sexual attention of any kind. These fears and anxieties are all unconscious. People suffering from eating disorders are not aware that they starve themselves, binge and purge, or exercise compulsively for reasons beyond being thin.

A mother explains a household rule to her daughter. Sometimes, parents can be overprotective of their children by not letting them learn to make their own decisions. Teens who feel that their relationship with food is one area that they can control may develop eating disorders because of family problems.

Social Factors

Americans live in a world where people, especially women, are often judged by their appearance. From Barbie dolls to music videos to fashion models, girls and women are surrounded by unrealistic and unattainable images of the female body. In American society, thin people are thought to be attractive, good, strong, desirable, and successful. Overweight people are often viewed as lazy, socially inept, stupid, undesirable, and lonely. Many experts believe that if there were not such an intense

Ballet dancing is one of many areas that stresses thinness and body shape. Ballerinas have a high risk of developing an eating disorder.

emphasis to be thin and physically fit in this culture, eating disorders would be very rare.

In addition, certain activities, such as modeling, cheerleading, and ballet dancing, emphasize thinness and body shape. So do certain sports, such as gymnastics, wrestling, figure skating, swimming, and running. People involved in any of these activities are at higher risk for eating disorders. These days, many coaches and dance instructors are well aware of the dangers of eating disorders, and they emphasize the importance of proper nutrition and healthy eating routines. But coaches and teachers who emphasize weight control can encourage eating disorders without realizing it.

Biological Factors

There seems to be a genetic element that makes some people vulnerable to eating disorders. Scientists have found that people with eating disorders may have too much, or too little, of certain hormones and neurotransmitters. Hormones and neurotransmitters are chemicals in our bodies that stimulate certain body functions and help keep our minds and bodies running smoothly. No one knows exactly how much of a person's eating disorder is caused by chemical or biological tendencies that he or she was born with. This area is the least understood in relation to eating disorders, but researchers are working to learn more.

Trigger Factors

Sometimes, an event in someone's life will trigger an eating disorder. A triggering event might be the end of a love relationship. Often it is the beginning of a time of great change, with a new set of expectations, such as graduation, a new school, or a new job. A devastating trauma such as rape, sexual abuse, or incest also can trigger an eating disorder.

Another common triggering factor is weight- or body-related comments from friends, parents, siblings, doctors, or coaches. Young people are very sensitive to what other people think about them, especially people they want to please. Your doctor may say, "You should lose ten pounds." Your coach might joke, "Better lay off the ice cream." But to you it's not funny. You may think, "I'm fat! I look terrible! I have to change the way I look!" The adult may not realize it, but comments about weight can

Coaches, trainers, and dance teachers who emphasize weight control can unknowingly cause a young person to develop an eating disorder.

trigger unhealthy eating and exercise habits, which could develop into an eating disorder.

No Single Cause

Many factors contribute to an eating disorder. The person who is experiencing it usually does not realize what's going on. It's not as if a person says, "My parents don't pay attention to me, so I'm going to punish them by losing weight." It's an unconscious process, which means it happens without a person's realizing it. Recovering from an eating disorder involves uncovering its causes and learning how to deal with those problems in a healthy way.

HOW CAN COMPULSIVE EXERCISE HURT ME?

Compulsive exercise, like all eating disorders, damages the body, the mind, and the spirit. The human body needs rest as much as it needs food and water. Even professional athletes do not train every day because they know that they must rest to stay strong and fit. Compulsive exercisers don't give their bodies enough time to recuperate. Because of this, they develop painful injuries, such as stress fractures and torn muscles, ligaments, tendons, and cartilage.

Food is our body's fuel. The more energy a person expends, the more fuel he or she needs. An athlete needs to eat more than a person who sits at a desk all day. Compulsive exercisers usually do not eat enough to sustain their high level of activity. Because they use many more calories than they take in, they become very weak and their bodies break down.

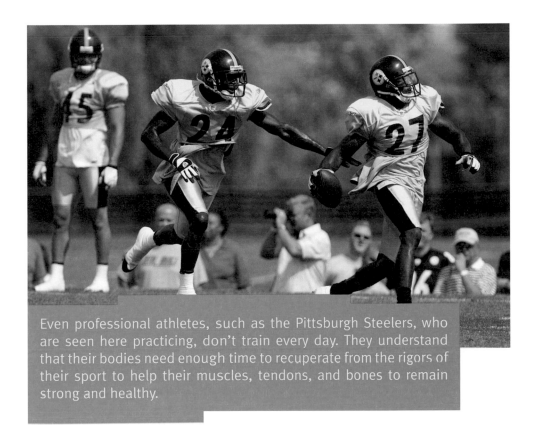

Even professional athletes, such as the Pittsburgh Steelers, who are seen here practicing, don't train every day. They understand that their bodies need enough time to recuperate from the rigors of their sport to help their muscles, tendons, and bones to remain strong and healthy.

All eating disorders cause serious physical problems. People with bulimia develop ulcers (holes or tears) in their stomachs, throats, and mouths because the gastric (stomach) acid the body uses to digest food is continually brought up through vomiting. Ulcers are very serious and painful and can be fatal. People who have bulimia often have yellow, damaged teeth. This condition is also caused by acids brought up into the mouth through repeated vomiting. The acids wear off the protective enamel on the teeth. People with bulimia also get painful stomach cramps from severe constipation. This problem is caused by the abuse of

Some eating disorders, such as bulimia, cause people to develop ulcers in their mouths and throats from too much vomiting. Bulimics can also have yellow, decayed teeth because of the acids brought up into the mouth during purging.

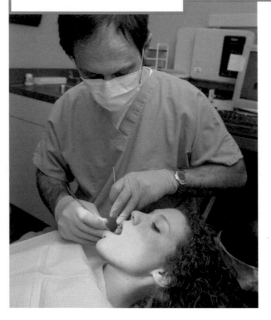

laxatives, which damages the digestive system. People with bulimia become weak and exhausted.

People with anorexia are always cold. Their hands and feet may look blue. This is because their bodies don't have enough fat to keep them warm. As a result, fine hairs, called lanugo, grow all over their bodies. A girl with anorexia stops producing estrogen (the female hormone), causing her bones to lose mass and weaken. When she gets older, she will be at high risk for osteoporosis. People with anorexia also suffer from painful stomach cramps because the body is physically straining to retain what little nutrition is available. Blood pressure and the heart rate slow down and weaken, so that the whole body is slower and weaker. These effects of starvation can result in death.

Women and girls with eating disorders stop getting their menstrual periods. As a girl recovers, the return of her period is a sign of her returning health.

Exercise addiction or having an eating disorder can take a physical as well as a psychological toll on a person. Compulsive exercisers feel increasingly isolated from their family and friends, and their self-image often leads them to unnatural thoughts.

As bad as the physical symptoms are, the emotional toll of an eating disorder can be even worse. As exercise takes up more and more time, compulsive exercisers become increasingly isolated. That isolation makes them more depressed and unhappy—then they may exercise even more to try to feel better. They have so little contact with other people that their self-image becomes increasingly distorted. They think that anyone who tries to help them is an enemy.

Exercise and diet can provide a temporary escape from stress and give us a feeling of control over our lives. But when diet and exercise become an obsession, they control you. Experts believe that eating disorders are as addictive as cocaine or alcohol. They can be just as dangerous as well. We actually can develop an addiction to our body's own chemicals when we develop an addiction to a behavior such as exercise. Endorphins that get released through exercise are the body's own "inner morphins" and are very similar to opiates, such as heroin. If you exercise too much, you can create tolerance to your own neurotransmitters, needing more and more to feel good. Just as with a drug addiction, you experience withdrawal symptoms when you stop the behavior, such as depression, irritability, and anxiety. This dynamic explains why people don't just get "psychologically" addicted to a behavior like exercise or gambling. There is a physical addiction happening at the same time that can contribute to the fact that it is so hard to stop.

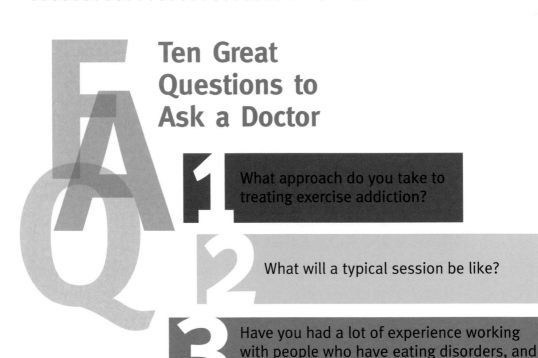

Ten Great Questions to Ask a Doctor

1 What approach do you take to treating exercise addiction?

2 What will a typical session be like?

3 Have you had a lot of experience working with people who have eating disorders, and specifically exercise addiction?

4 What causes exercise addiction?

5 How long do you think the treatment process will be?

6 How often will I see you, and can I call you between sessions if I feel I need to?

7 Do you believe in using medication to treat eating disorders?

8 Does exercise addiction cause other health problems, and will I need to go to more than one kind of doctor?

9 What nutritional information will I receive when I begin treatment for exercise addiction?

10 If I feel like I'm not improving fast enough, what can I do? How do you deal with relapses or slow progress?

HOW DO I GET HELP?

Many young people will develop an eating disorder at some point in their lives. It may be in junior high, in high school, or in their early twenties.

Recovery from an eating disorder is not easy. Between 20 and 30 percent of people who enter treatment either drop out before they recover or relapse after they leave treatment. It takes major commitments to start treatment, continue treatment, make the necessary changes in lifestyle, and deal with the underlying psychological and emotional issues that led to the eating disorder in the first place. But it is possible: eight out of ten people who enter treatment for eating disorders either recover completely or at least make significant progress.

The treatment for an eating disorder includes several elements. In severe cases, hospitalization is required to prevent death, suicide, or some kind of medical crisis.

To get help with her eating disorder, this teen attended the Renfrew Center, a clinic for eating disorders in Coconut Creek, Florida. Her eating disorder symptoms were limiting the amount of food she ate and compulsive exercise, which included competitive swimming.

Restoration of a healthy and consistent weight is a goal. Medication may be prescribed to relieve depression and anxiety. Patients whose eating disorder has led to damaged teeth may require dental work. And finally, there is counseling: individual counseling to help the patient take control of his or her own life in a healthy way; group counseling to help patients learn how to manage their relationships effectively; family counseling to create new, healthy patterns of family life; body-centered psychotherapy to develop a healthy body image; and nutritional counseling to help patients learn the truth about healthy eating habits and help them design proper meals. Many patients will also join support groups to help ease feelings of isolation and alienation.

Even with treatment, recovery is a slow process. Only a few people recover from an eating disorder in a year or less. For most people, it takes three to seven years, and for some people it takes even longer. However, the most intensive period of therapy is at the very beginning of treatment, when there may be several sessions every week and even time spent in the hospital. As progress is made, therapy sessions become less frequent.

Recovering from an eating disorder is like fighting an addiction to drugs or alcohol. It is a long, slow, difficult process, and it may never be 100 percent complete. A recovering alcoholic will always have to be careful—even if he or she hasn't had a drink in years. During periods of stress, he or she may have a strong urge to drink. Although people with a drug or alcohol addiction can recover and choose to stay away from the substance they are addicted to, people with eating disorders need to find a healthy relationship with food or exercise, meaning they have to make friends with the issue they have the most trouble with because staying away or avoiding it is not an option. People with eating disorders will also have ongoing struggles and may relapse many times.

How to Help

How do you find counselors or physicians you trust and can work with effectively? Here are some tips:

- If you're in a crisis situation, call 9-1-1 or a crisis hotline; they're usually listed in the yellow pages under "Crisis intervention." Or go to a hospital emergency room and tell the staff what's going on.
- Ask your family doctor to evaluate you and refer you to a counselor. Don't be embarrassed: doctors and counselors have dealt with many cases of eating disorders before.
- Ask people you trust who have been in your situation for the names of physicians and counselors they found helpful.
- If you are a student, your school counseling center, nurse, coach, or guidance counselor may be able to help you or point you to someone who can.
- If you have little money or your health insurance doesn't cover treatment for eating disorders, look under "Counselors" in the yellow pages for community service organizations. They may not have formal eating disorder programs, but they offer basic assistance.

These health professionals are working at a call center for a teen helpline at a hospital in California. Teens needing help with eating disorders or addiction can call crisis hotlines, doctors, counselors, or clinics for treatment information.

Remember, recovery is possible. Many healthy and active people have struggled with an eating disorder at some point in their lives. The important thing is to recognize your problem and get help.

I Have This Friend . . .

You may have a friend you think is struggling with compulsive exercise, anorexia, or bulimia. How you respond to the problem can make a big difference in his or her recovery. But remember, you cannot control another person's behavior. You cannot force your friend to exercise less or eat more. You can, however, express your concern and offer your support. Here are some tips for helping.

Try to do the following:

→ Speak to your friend privately.
→ Tell your friend you're concerned about him or her because you care about him or her.
→ Be prepared that your friend will deny that he or she has a problem. Your friend may get angry or hostile toward you.

Remember that it's not up to you. You can support and encourage your friend, but you can't make him or her recover if your friend is not ready to.

Try *not* to do the following:

→ Speak to anyone else about your friend before you talk with him or her. Don't bring a group of friends along to confront him or her.
→ Tell your friend he or she is doing something "crazy," "sick," or "wrong."
→ Give your friend advice about exercise, diet, or his or her appearance.
→ Plead, beg, threaten, or get into an argument with your friend. Try not to get into a power struggle.
→ Pry or spy. Don't try to be the "Food Police." Your friend will just resent you and become even more secretive.

Before you speak to your friend, write down the name and phone number or the Internet address of an eating disorder organization. After you express your concern and listen to what he or she has to say, offer that phone number. You can try saying, "Why don't you take the number? That way, if you ever want to call, you'll have it." But remember, you can't force your friend to get help. He or she has to want help and be ready to accept it.

In general, it is better to speak directly to your friend before you speak to anyone else about him or her. There is an exception. If you believe your friend is in serious danger, you should tell someone right away. Some signs of danger are if your friend is throwing up more than once each day, is throwing up blood, has a very severe stomachache, or expresses suicidal thoughts. These are emergency situations. Tell an adult whom you trust as soon as possible.

Things to Remember

Remember some of the following key symptoms of being a person who may be addicted to exercise or have an eating disorder:

- Exercise isn't fun or it makes you feel worse, instead of better.
- You think about your exercise routine all of the time and always feel that you should be doing more.
- You keep a list of what you are allowed to eat and only let yourself eat certain amounts of food.

Remember that your value as a person is not reflected in a mirror or by the numbers on a scale. You have the power to change your feelings, actions, and thoughts. You also have the power to learn to accept yourself. It might be a lifelong journey, but it is one definitely worth traveling.

- You've lost weight, and people tell you you're thin, but you still want to lose more.
- You think about your body and your weight all of the time.
- You do things to lose weight that you do not tell anybody about.

It can be a serious problem, but it can be overcome. If someone you care about has an eating disorder or is addicted to exercise, share the information you have learned about the condition. If you think you may have a problem, please speak to someone about it. You deserve to get more out of life. You are not what you weigh, and your value as a human being is not reflected in the numbers on a scale.

addiction An obsessive or compulsive need for and use of a substance or a behavior.

biological Based in your body.

body image The way you see yourself and how you think others see you.

bulimia A disorder in which overeating (bingeing) alternates with trying to get rid of the food (purging) so that there is no weight gain. Purging can be done by self-induced vomiting; abuse of laxatives, diet pills, or diuretics; excessive exercise; or fasting.

calorie A unit of energy that food provides.

compulsive Relating to feeling psychologically unable to resist performing or doing things.

constipation The inability to have a bowel movement, causing cramps, stomachaches, and gas.

depression Feelings of sadness and hopelessness that last for a long period of time.

discipline Self-control; the ability to stick to a certain routine, behavior, or activity.

distorted Warped; not based in reality.

dopamine A neurotransmitter that your body releases when you challenge yourself, for example, through exercise. You need a healthy supply of dopamine to feel energy, motivation, and confidence. However, you can get addicted to your own dopamine through behavior addictions, such as exercise, gambling, sex, or criminal behaviors.

eating disorder An unhealthy and extreme concern with weight, body size, food, and eating habits.

endorphins The body's "inner morphins," chemicals your body releases when you move beyond the pain threshold in order to numb pain. They also create feelings of elation, happiness, and contentment.

estrogen A female hormone.

fasting Not eating for a whole day or more.

genetic Relating to the qualities or tendencies that we are born with.

hormones Substances formed in certain glands that control body processes, such as growth.

immune system The body's system for protecting itself from disease and infection.

laxative A pill or liquid that brings on a bowel movement.

metabolism The processes by which the body turns food into energy.

neurotransmitters The body's own chemicals (such as endorphins, dopamine, and serotonin) that people have to transmit information in the nervous system, especially in regards to their emotions.

nutrients Vitamins, minerals, and other food ingredients that your body needs to stay healthy.

nutrition What and how we eat to nourish and maintain a healthy body.

obsession A persistent and disturbing preoccupation with an unhealthy or unreasonable idea or feeling.

perfectionist Someone who is never satisfied with his or her own performance, appearance, grades, or other achievements; someone who believes that anything less than perfection is failure.

psychological Having to do with the inner workings of the mind; mental.

puberty The time when your body becomes sexually mature.

purge To get rid of food suddenly and harshly, usually by vomiting, exercise, or laxatives.

self-esteem Self-respect; satisfaction with oneself.

self-image How a person sees and thinks of herself or himself.

testosterone A male hormone.

trauma An event in a person's life that is highly disruptive, very negative, and life-changing.

About-Face

P.O. Box 77665

San Francisco, CA 94107

(415) 436-0212

Web site: http://www.about-face.org

> About-Face promotes positive self-esteem in girls and women of all ages, sizes, races, and backgrounds through a spirited approach to media education, outreach, and activism.

The Alliance for Eating Disorders Awareness

P.O. Box 13155

North Palm Beach, FL 33408-3155

(866) 662-1235

Web site: http://www.eatingdisorderinfo.org

> This organization tries to establish easily accessible programs in the United States that allow children and young adults the opportunity to learn about eating disorders and the positive effects of a healthy body image. Its aim is to disseminate educational information to the public about the warning signs, dangers, and consequences of anorexia, bulimia, and other related disorders, including exercise addiction. The alliance also works to educate individuals, especially teenagers, about the dangers of eating disorders.

Anorexia Nervosa and Related Eating Disorders, Inc. (ANRED)
P.O. Box 5102
Eugene, OR 97405
(541) 344-1144
Web site: http://www.anred.com

ANRED is a nonprofit organization, founded in 1979, that wants to make it easier for people to learn about eating disorders and how to recover from them. Officers include a psychiatrist, a clinical psychologist, a psychiatric nurse practitioner, a registered nurse who works in a mental health agency, and a pastoral counselor/eating disorders specialist.

National Association of Anorexia Nervosa and Associated
    Disorders (ANAD)
P.O. Box 7
Highland Park, IL 60035
(847) 831-3438
Web site: http://www.anad.org

ANAD was founded in 1976 and is the oldest eating disorder organization in the United States. Its president and founder, Vivian Meehan, was a nurse at a hospital in Highland Park, Illinois, when her daughter developed anorexia nervosa and she discovered there was no information available for sufferers or families and no support systems. Today, ANAD answer thousands of hotline calls each year and continues to assist individuals and their families to find resources and provide referrals to professionals.

National Eating Disorders Association (NEDA)
603 Stewart Street, Suite 803
Seattle, WA 98101
(800) 931-2237
Web site: http://www.nationaleatingdisorders.org
  NEDA works to prevent eating disorders and provide treatment
  referrals to those suffering from anorexia, bulimia, and binge
  eating disorder, and those concerned with body image and
  weight issues.

S.A.F.E. Alternatives (Self-Abuse Finally Ends)
40 Timberline Drive
Lemont, IL 60439
(800) 669-2426
Information line: (800) 366-8288
Web site: http://www.selfinjury.com
  S.A.F.E. Alternatives (Self-Abuse Finally Ends) is a nationally
  recognized treatment approach, professional network, and
  educational resource base that is committed to helping
  people achieve an end to self-injurious behavior.

Web Sites

Due to the changing nature of Internet links, Rosen Publishing
has developed an online list of Web sites related to the subject
of this book. This site is updated regularly. Please use this link
to access the list:

http://www.rosenlinks.com/faq/exad

For Further Reading

Andersen, Arnold, Leigh Cohn, and Tom Holbrook. *Making Weight: Healing Men's Conflicts with Food, Weight, and Shape*. Carlsbad, CA: Gurze Books, 2000.

Arnold, Carrie, and B. Timothy Walsh. *Next to Nothing: A Firsthand Account of One Teenager's Experience with an Eating Disorder*. New York, NY: Oxford University Press, 2007.

Bell, Julia. *Massive*. New York, NY: Simon Pulse, 2005.

Cirrone, Dorian. *Dancing in Red Shoes Will Kill You*. New York, NY: HarperCollins, 2005.

Fitzhugh, Karla. *Body Image*. Orlando, FL: Steck-Vaughn, 2004.

Gay, Kathlyn. *Eating Disorders—Anorexia, Bulimia, and Binge Eating*. Berkeley Heights, NJ: Enslow Publishers, 2003.

Greenfield, Lauren. *Thin*. San Francisco, CA: Chronicle Books, 2006.

Hinds, Maurene J. *Focus on Body Image: How You Feel About How You Look*. Berkely Heights, NJ: Enslow Publishers, 2002.

Kalodner, Cynthia R. *Too Fat or Too Thin? A Reference Guide to Eating Disorders*. Carmarthen, UK: Crown House Publishing, 2005.

Kaslik, Ibi. *Skinny*. New York, NY: Walker Books for Young Readers, 2006.

Kingsbury, Kathleen Burns, and Mary Ellen Williams. *Weight Wisdom*. New York, NY: Taylor and Francis, 2003.

Kirberger, Kimberly. *No Body's Perfect: Stories by Teens About Body Image, Self-Acceptance, and the Search for Identity.* New York, NY: Scholastic, 2003.

Lawton, Sandra Augustyn, ed. *Eating Disorders Information for Teens: Health Tips About Anorexia, Bulimia, Binge Eating, and Other Eating Disorders*. Detroit. MI: Omnigraphics, 2005.

Litt, Ann. *Fuel for Young Athletes: Essential Foods and Fluids for Future Champions*. Champaign, IL: Human Kinetics, 2004.

Mackler, Carolyn. *The Earth, My Butt, and Other Big Round Things*. Cambridge, MA: Candlewick Press, 2003.

Ojeda, Auriana, ed. *Body Image* (Teen Decision). San Diego, CA: Greenhaven Press, 2002.

Orr, Tamra B. *When the Mirror Lies: Anorexia, Bulimia, and Other Eating Disorders*. New York, NY: Franklin Watts, 2006.

Otis, Carol L., and Roger Goldingay. *The Athletic Woman's Survival Guide: How to Win the Battle Against Eating Disorders, Amenorrhea, and Osteoporosis*. Champaign, IL: Human Kinetics, 2000.

Phillips, Katherine A. *The Broken Mirror: Understanding and Treating Body Dysmorphic Disorder*. Rev. ed. New York, NY: Oxford University Press, 2005.

Pope, Harrison G., Jr., Katharine A. Phillips, and Roberto Olivardia. *The Adonis Complex: The Secret Crisis of Male Body Obsession*. New York, NY: Free Press, 2000.

Ryerson, Margi. *Appetite for Life: Inspiring Stories of Recovery from Anorexia, Bulimia, and Compulsive Overeating*. Lincoln, NE: iUniverse, 2005.

Salmon, Margaret B. *Food Facts for Teenagers: A Guide to Good Nutrition for Teens and Preteens.* 2nd ed. Springfield, IL: Charles C. Thomas, 2003.

Schlosser, Eric. *Chew on This: Everything You Don't Want to Know About Fast Food.* Boston, MA: Houghton Mifflin, 2006.

Sparks, Beatrice. *Kim: Empty Inside.* New York, NY: Avon, 2002.

Stromberg, Gary, and Jane Merrill. *Feeding the Fame: Celebrities Tell Their Real-life Stories of Eating Disorders and Recovery.* Center City, MN: Hazelden Publishing and Educational Services, 2006.

Vrettos, Adrienne Maria. *Skin.* New York, NY: Margaret K. McElderry Books, 2006.

Whytock, Cherry. *My Cup Runneth Over: The Life of Angelica Cookson Potts.* New York, NY: Simon and Schuster, 2003.

Index

About the Author

Edward Willett is the author of nonfiction books for young adults on the subjects of meningitis, arthritis, hemophilia, Alzheimer's disease, and genetics. He has also written articles on topics related to eating disorders, including body dysmorphic disorder, negative body image, and weight and depression for Rosen Publishing's Teen Health and Wellness database. Willett lives in Regina, Saskatchewan, Canada, where he writes a weekly science column for newspapers and radio.

Photo Credits

Cover © www.istockphoto.com/Ken Hurst; p. 5 © www.istockphoto.com/heinz linke; p. 8 © plainpicture GmbH & Co. KG/Alamy; p. 11 © www.istockphoto.com/Sharon Dominick; p. 14 © www.istockphoto.com/Dawna Stafford; p. 18 © www.istockphoto.com/eva serrabassa; pp. 22, 51 © Shutterstock.com; p. 25 © www.istockphoto.com/Amanda Rohde; p. 27 © Ed Young/AGStockUSA, Inc./Alamy; p. 31 © www.istockphoto.com/Ana Blazic; p. 33 © www.istockphoto.com/cjmckendry; pp. 34, 48 © AP Images; p. 36 © www.istockphoto.com/Francisco Orellana; p. 39 © Gregory Shamus/Getty Images; p. 40 © www.istockphoto.com/David Lewis; p. 41 © www.istockphoto.com/Liz Van Steenburgh; p. 45 © Lauren Greenfield/VII/AP Images.

Designer: Evelyn Horovicz; Editor: Kathy Kuhtz Campbell
Photo Researcher: Amy Feinberg